Summary of

Red Notice

by Bill Browder

Instaread

Please Note

This is an unofficial summary and analysis.

Table of Contents

Summary

Red Notice: A True Story of High Finance, Murder, and One Man's Fight for Justice by Bill Browder is a unique story that blends biography, entrepreneurial business narrative, history, true crime, and a human rights crusade all into one book.

Browder's grandfather was the leader of the American Communist Party. For Browder, going to business school and trying to be a capitalist was a good way to rebel against his liberal parents. After earning his master's of business administration (MBA), however, the standard post business school paths failed to inspire him. His grandfather had spent a lot of time in Eastern Europe and made a name for himself there. Young Browder thought if his grandfather could find fame and distinction there, so could he.

Lucky for Browder, he graduated in 1989, the same year the Berlin Wall came down, leading to the end of the Cold War. For a United States citizen who wanted to do business in Eastern Europe, the time was right. At the time, however, everyone thought Browder was crazy.

Yet, Browder was determined. At his first job, he ended up being the point-man for a Polish consulting project he found disheartening. However, he did invest two thousand dollars of his own money in the new Polish stock market and, by the end of the next year, his investment had increased tenfold. Now he knew what he wanted to do. He wanted to invest in Eastern Europe. He described the ensuing high from his discovery and profit as the greatest feeling he had ever had.

Eventually, working for a new company, Browder went to Russia, the one place his coworkers would not touch, leaving it completely open to him. At his first job there, he would find that privatization in Russia was a potential gold mine to which nobody was paying any attention. The fishing company he was advising was incredibly undervalued, and he decided to find out how common this was. During his investigations, Browder discovered that the Russian government, in the transition from communism to capitalism, had allocated about thirty percent of the Russian economy to be distributed to citizens through vouchers, and that the entire Russian economy, which was sitting on rich natural resource reserves, was obscenely undervalued. Perhaps most significant of all, there was no regulation on who could buy the public vouchers.

Browder acted on this information and ended up making his company a lot of money, but the company tried to muscle him out of his own business. He eventually broke out on his own, founding his company, Hermitage Capital. Browder convinced one of the world's most celebrated financiers, Edmond Safra, to back him as a partner with a twenty-five million dollar investment in exchange for a fifty percent stake in the new company. They were able to buy large numbers of the vouchers, research large Russian companies that were incredibly undervalued, and make a killing in profits.

Business took off, but the first truly jaw-dropping break-through happened when Browder discovered a Russian oil company, Sidanco, was trading at six times less than the famous Russian company Yukoil and at sixty times less than British Petroleum (BP), both of which also had comparable oil reserves. Browder bought one and two tenths of a percent of the four percent publicly available for about eleven million dollars. About a year later, in 1997, BP bought ten percent of the company owner's shares for a price six hundred percent higher than what Browder had paid, blowing his profit sky high.

Yet, the Russian oligarch who controlled Sidanco wanted to squeeze Hermitage Capital out of its profits, trying to split the shares of all shareholders except for Hermitage Capital, dramatically devaluing its holdings. Hermitage Capital went to war with the oligarch, a dangerous move because taking on Russian oligarchs could often prove fatal. However, Browder reached out to the international media and convinced investors that they could be next. The Russian government finally intervened and stopped the splitting of the stock.

In just a few years, Browder had taken the initial twenty-five million dollars and turned it into over a billion, and his fund was named the best in the world in 1997. The 1998 financial crisis wiped most of this out, and by 1999, the same year Safra died in a mysterious fire, most

Western investors had bailed on Russia. This meant that a major check against financial or economic abuse by oligarchs was removed.

Abuse became so bad that investors just assumed most companies were corrupt and their assets were being robbed, with large portions given away to owners' friends and family. Undervaluation was common. With creative research methods, and starting with Russia's giant oil and gas company Gazprom, Browder was able to discover exactly how much was being stolen and by whom. With his investments into Gazprom and other, similar companies, Hermitage Capital was able to make a comeback when his investigations revealed to the public the true value of these companies. For a time, the new Russian president, Vladimir Putin, was looking to tame the oligarchs himself, and Browder was free to pursue his profit-making, corruption-busting crusade. Plus, Browder was confident that, as a foreigner in Russia, he would be safe. This worked for a while. However, once Putin had the oligarchs in line, things changed. On arriving in Russia late in 2005, Browder was detained and eventually deported. He was deemed a threat to national security. Browder eventually discovered that this went all the way up to Russia's Federal Security Service (FSB), the successor to the dreaded *Komitet gosudarstvennoy bezopasnosti,* or Committee for State Security (KGB), of the Soviet Union's secret police, and possibly as high a Putin and his inner-circle.

Browder was losing many clients and began to move his money and people out of Russian investments. At one point, he received a call from Lieutenant Colonel Artem Kuznetsov in what appeared to be an attempt to solicit a bribe. Browder ignored him.

A few months later, Kuznetsov showed up with dozens of police officers and began illegally seizing materials from Hermitage Capital's Moscow office, taking almost everything he could. Soon after, Hermitage Capital's partners and clients were similarly raided. A lawyer who pointed out the illegality of the Russian warrants was beaten up. The man was also falsely charged with tax evasion in relation to a company owned by one of Hermitage Capital's clients, but the officers took information that had nothing to do with the case. Sergei Magnitsky, a very successful tax lawyer from a partner firm, investigated the tax allegations and found no wrongdoing after examining all of the relevant documents. Another lawyer went to the Interior Ministry to confront authorities there, and came across the man running the investigation, Major Pavel Karpov, who illegally denied access to the case files.

This was the beginning of a massive conspiracy involving Russian authorities spread out across various agencies. Kuznetsov and Pavel together used the files they had seized in their raids to forge documents to sell parts of Hermitage Capital to associates. With these stolen parts of Hermitage Capital, they claimed the parts were operating at a loss, with losses in 2007 equal to Hermitage Capital's profits for the year 2006. Due to these losses, the Russians could claim a tax rebate to the tune of two hundred and thirty million dollars. All this happened unbeknownst to Browder.

Magnitsky figured out what was happening with Hermitage Capital, and that the charges against Browder were just a way for Kuznetsov and Pavel to steal money from the Russian taxpayers using his documents. Over time, Browder and his team were able to prove it by tracing large amounts of money going into bank accounts related to Kuznetsov, Pavel, and their families, as well as the tax officials who had approved the rebate. On the small salary of Russian bureaucrats, these people owned things like expensive cars and houses worth millions, and traveled all around the world. Browder and his team exposed all this information on popular YouTube videos in Russian and English, generating a backlash in Russia among the public and garnered media attention worldwide.

The Russian authorities did not take Browder's response to the thefts of Hermitage Capital passively. They put pressure on Browder's people in Russia to the point that they all had to flee. Eventually only Sergei Magnitsky remained. He was arrested and falsely charged in 2008. He refused to recant, and became sick while in custody. He was systematically denied medical treatment and tortured. Even during court appearances he remained defiant as his health dramatically worsened. In November 2009, he was beaten to death by prison guards. The Russian authorities came up with all kinds of inconsistent and changing stories, making their guilt obvious. They tried Magnitsky and convicted him after his death, a first in Russian history. They also tried and convicted Browder in absentia.

The quest for justice failed in Russia, but succeeded in the United States and Europe. Against the odds, Browder got a law passed in the US Congress, named the Magnitsky Act, that publicly named the officials responsible for Magnitsky's murder, denied them visas, and froze their assets, and made those who committed similar abuses subject to it. The European Parliament passed a similar law. Though Browder felt his life was in danger and, in part, lived like a wanted man as other prominent critics of Putin have ended up dead, he made it known that the biggest rush in his life was not the rush of finding that great deal in Poland all those years back, but in getting laws passed to punish those who killed Magnitsky and to protect others who face similar abuse by the Putin regime in Moscow.

Important People

Bill Browder: Bill Browder is the author and main character in this book. It is Browder's dream of being the first big Western businessman to operate in Eastern Europe and his establishment of Hermitage Capital in Moscow that sets the stage for the entire story of the book.

Edmond Safra: Edmond Safra was Browder's founding and main business partner in Hermitage Capital. He was one of the most famous financiers on the globe, but died in a strange fire in his home in Monaco.

Sergei Magnitsky: Sergei Magnitsky was one of several lawyers operating in Russia on behalf of Hermitage Capital. Magnitsky's arrest, detention, torture, and death at the hands of Russian authorities dominates the last third of the book.

Artem Kuznetsov: Artem Kuznetsov was a lieutenant colonel in Russia's Interior Ministry who at first solicited a bribe from Browder. He then used his position to enrich himself by millions at the expense of Browder, Hermitage Capital, and the Russian taxpayers by opening up investigations on false charges against Browder, his associates, and partners.

Pavel Karpov: Pavel Karpov was a major in the Russian Interior Ministry who was working with Karpov as the lead investigator of Brower. Karpov, like Kuznetsov, benefited enormously from his corruption and illegal activity.

Analysis

Key Takeaways

Key Takeaway 1

The business world was ruthless even outside of Russia.

Analysis

Early in the book, Browder gets a crash course in the business world that is a baptism by fire. One of the first jobs Browder had was working for Robert Maxwell, a man notorious for his hard and cruel treatment of his employees. When Maxwell died in an accident at sea, it was revealed soon after that he robbed the payroll and pension funds to inflate his own stock price in the biggest fraud in British history. Most of the employees were fired, showing how selfishness and greed could play out into cruelty and lost savings. When Browder moved to Salomon Brothers, no one wanted to let him in on any of the company's existing business and he was forced to strike out largely on his own, showing how selfish many people in high-profile companies could be. When he finally succeeded in Russia, Browder realized Salomon Brothers was trying to push him both out of getting credit he deserved and out of running the new Russian operations, demonstrating that even when a person performed well, just treatment was far from guaranteed. Finally, when Browder negotiated a contract to set up Hermitage Capital with US billionaire Ron Burkle, Burkle tried to impose unfair terms on Browder, showing that even those who already had a major advantage were often looking to press for even more of an advantage at the expense of weaker parties.

Key Takeaway 2

The business world was all about connections.

Analysis

Throughout the entire book, a constant truth is that connections matter a great deal. A huge portion of Browder's big business deals and breaks come from his connection to someone who was able to set up a meeting or help seal a deal. This was how Browder was introduced to Safra, it was how he was able to crash the events at, and begin his annual experiences at, the World Economic Forum in Davos, and it was how he was able to meet US Senator John McCain. Reporters he befriended were able to give him advance notice about crucial developments, and his network in Moscow and Stanford also served him well. Without the connections he did have, it is hard for the reader to imagine Browder being as successful as he was. The key was that he had to work hard to earn the ability to become acquainted with certain people, and those people often opened doors for him to meet much more influential people.

Key Takeaway 3

Knowledge was power and research was sometimes better than cash.

Analysis

At several key junctures in the book, Browder was a pioneer going where no, or few, Westerners had gone before. He broke into territory that was brand new for several of his companies and was the driving force behind even getting them to consider those directions. In each one of those situations, Browder got the jump on all his coworkers, competitors, and his whole industry by seeking out hard to find information in person and by thinking about applying this information creatively in a way no one else seemed to have done before him. More than any other single factor, this was what propelled him to fame and fortune. Browder seemed to have been the first Westerner to realize how undervalued the post-Soviet Russian economy was. Whether looking into Sidanco, Lukoil, or Gazprom, Browder looked at them from angles that previous investors had missed and was able to exclusively apply this information in ways that rewarded his investors. It was this research that got him his connection to the person who would introduce him to Safra and that convinced Safra to put up Hermitage Capital's initial twenty-five million dollars. It was this research that enabled Browder to turn twenty-five million dollars into one billion dollars and have Hermitage Capital named the best fund of the year in 1997. Such research also enabled him to uncover and fight massive amounts of corruption in Russia, and, finally, it enabled him to stay several steps ahead of his far less creative Russian government tricksters. He was able to get back at them with public information and legal campaigns that took the fight to them. Ultimately, his superior knowledge and research skills did much to enable him to win his fight to achieve a measure of justice for Magnitsky, and it was the same research that demonstrated how overwhelmingly legitimate his case was and how overwhelmingly illegitimate the case of the Russian state was.

Key Takeaway 4

Problems spread in a global economy.

Analysis

Perhaps the single worst decision on the part of Browder was to believe the Asian economic crises in 1997 would not have a huge impact on Russia. The main thing he missed was that a bad performance for investors in one area will create panic with other, riskier investments in a separate sector. In this case, that separate sector was Russia. Due to this incorrect assumption on Browder's part, when he assured nervous investors and his partners that Russia would be immune from the pain going on in Asia, Hermitage Capital lost nine hundred million dollars out of its billion dollars in assets. While Browder's marriages were never the main story here, it was telling that his first marriage ended at the time these losses were incurred. The most difficult time of his life to this point was digging himself and his investors out of this hole because he failed to anticipate the ripple-effect of the nature of modern economies.

Key Takeaway 5

With every problem there was an opportunity. Resilience could pay off.

Analysis

All throughout this story, Browder was able to tackle problems and create opportunities. His dogged effort paid off repeatedly. It was working for the disaster of Maxwell when Browder made his connection that would get him into Davos and the World Economic Forum. It was Salomon Brothers trying to take over and take credit for what Browder had built that got Browder to cast off on his own and develop Hermitage Capital. It was Burkle's unsavory dealings that helped Browder seal the deal to create Hermitage Capital with Safra. Browder's fight with Sidanco showed his investors he could stand up to the Russian oligarchs and got him even more business. The 1998 meltdown of the Russian economy forced him to engage in more research to rebuild Hermitage Capital's assets, and this led to him figuring out the corrupt schemes of the oligarchs and taking them on successfully. Finally, the whole crisis with Putin's government and Magnitsky propelled Browder into the role of human rights crusader, helping him to advance justice for thousands of Russians and, since the Magnitsky Act is being used presently in Ukraine, for thousands of Ukrainians also. In each case, it would have been easy for Browder to pack his bags, go home, give in to his enemy, or give up. In each case, he did not and, instead, accomplished great things because he did not give up. Thus, an essential combination for success in business and in life is to meet setbacks and problems with determination.

Key Takeaway 6

To operate in Putin's Russia, it was necessary to know the limits of official engagement.

Analysis

One thing that was unique about Browder's experience in Russia was that he both experienced a beneficial relationship with the government and a lethal one. Due to these two extremes, Browder's tale is uniquely instructive as to the limits of official government engagement in Russia under the leadership of Putin. The trick seemed to be to know when the Russian government's interests coincided with whatever was at stake.

When Browder brought a lot of attention to Sidanco's bullying of Hermitage Capital to both the global media and to Western investors active in and considering investment in Russia, the Russian government intervened to stop the exclusionary stock split that singled out Hermitage Capital because this action had the potential to scare off foreign investors at a time when foreign investors were pumping a lot of money into the Russian economy. When the Russian economy collapsed and Western investors fled the Russian scene, there was no longer the same incentive to police the oligarchs' behavior in terms of retaining

Western investment. However, there was an incentive for Putin to use Browder's battles with the oligarchs to take them down a notch and to assert his own control over them. When Putin accomplished this, there was little incentive for Putin's regime to protect Browder anymore against his newly tamed allies. Therefore, it should be no surprise that Browder was seen as disposable by Putin and should not even be surprising that the Russian government turned on him.

Key Takeaway 7

Anything in Russia was difficult. A person needed to know how to find what they needed in order to operate in Russia.

Analysis

Knowing something in Russia is extremely difficult. For one thing, as the entire book makes clear, people are very reluctant to either answer direct questions or give direct answers. Decades of severely repressive rule and secret police hauling those who were direct and who shared too much information to gulags helped both weed out those whose personalities were more straightforward and scare others into avoiding such behavior. Even simple details on the assets of a company or a police investigation are hard to come by and are not given freely. Much like astronomers can find a black hole not by seeing it, but by seeing things around it pulled towards it, the truth in Russia is something that is often discovered indirectly by fleshing out details on related subjects that will reveal more about the subject in question or from an indirect source.

For Browder, finding out how much was stolen from a company helped him to ascertain that company's real value. An obscure trade magazine had more information on a company's assets than the company's own office, reporters had more information for him on the Russian authorities' investigations of him than the police themselves, and a boy selling stolen CD-ROMs in traffic had more information on company ownership in Moscow than any public directory. Browder's knack for exploring indirect and unconventional means for finding out what he needed, something he almost certainly was not taught at Stanford Business School, but was, rather, something intuitive on his part, was essential in his progress throughout these years.

Key Takeaway 8

There was no rule of law in Russia.

Analysis

Browder, towards the end of his narrative, points out that in Russia, it is not laws that rule, but men. When Putin and government officials wanted to go against the laws on the books, they were easily swept away, either by blatantly ignoring them or by concocting lies. That was how Browder was deemed a threat to national security. That was how a trial could be conducted in absentia or for someone who was dead. That was how authorities could give conflicting and changing accounts of how Magnitsky died, and how they could charge lawyers with crimes for simply doing their jobs. It was how police arrested anyone they could at the scene of a crime or beat up a lawyer who talked about rights or took materials from individuals that did not even pertain to an investigation. It was how authorities could falsify charges about tax crimes while using the charges to perpetrate tax crimes themselves, or bring about libel charges in a foreign court when they themselves were committing libel. It was how authorities could ignore Russian government documents that disproved their claims and continued a groundless investigation anyway. It was how a lawyer who had broken no laws could systematically be denied medical care, access to legal materials, family contact to which he was entitled, and be beaten to death. It was how such things were commonplace in Russia and there was little mass resistance.

In Russia, the law was not there to protect citizens and people, it was there to aid the authorities. The law was not meant to be used by citizens, but by the state.

Key Takeaway 9

The Russian authorities' Achilles' heel was their sloppiness.

Analysis

One of the most amazing takeaways from this is story is the sloppiness, lack of care, and how much contempt the Russian authorities have for public opinion that is displayed throughout the book. The Interior Ministry crooks, Kuznetsov and Karpov, who were cheating the government of two hundred and thirty million dollars barely attempted to launder the money, siphoning it off through their families' own personal accounts. They lived ostentatiously with expensive clothes and watches, partied at posh Moscow nightclubs, and went on exotic vacations to exclusive locations. None of this would have been possible on a normal civil servant's salary, and they made no attempt to even try to mask the fact that they were living like rock stars. They felt secure because of their positions of authority and their friends in high places. They just did not care to even try and cover their tracks.

This tendency was displayed in so many ways. Kuznetsov and Karpov did not try to come up with credible fake charges against Browder and his people, never mind even trying to avoid charging them with similar or the same crimes they themselves were committing. They did not bother to check to see if other relevant governmental departments had records proving the charges they were bringing against Browder and his associates were false and could exonerate the defendants. They did not care that they denied access to information that Browder's attorneys were legally entitled to see, or that they illegally summoned Browder's attorneys for illegal questioning. They did not care that their police officers beat up a lawyer who pointed out the illegality of their warrant and sent him into the hospital. Finally, they did not blink at having an associate charge Browder with libel in a United Kingdom court when they themselves were doing the same to Browder in a Russian court. The words total impunity come to mind when describing such actions.

This behavior went much farther than interior ministry officials. Judges who proclaimed sham verdicts and denied Magnistky's requests for medical attention or proper procedure were also guilty. So were many others. The doctors and nurses who refused him treatment in prison even though he had become gravely ill while in custody were guilty. The prison officials who denied Magnitsky contact with his family illegally, or illegally denied him access to the legal information about his case he was entitled to know were guilty. The press secretaries who repeated lie after lie were guilty. The governmental bodies that awarded these officials and/or decline to investigate them, or whose investigations exonerated them, or those who stopped legitimate government and independent investigations were guilty. The guards who beat him to death were guilty. The officials who would not allow his family to perform an independent autopsy were guilty. There was not even an attempt to coordinate the stories about how Magnitsky died or even what time he died, as various people gave conflicting statements and stories. Not even bothering to coordinate on the phony cause of death was, perhaps, the ultimate form of contempt for Magnitsky, his family, and public. There were many others involved in the whole sordid affair that were not mentioned here, as well.

Basically, Russian authorities just did not expect any consequences whatsoever, so they did not even think it important to have a solid fake story.

Key Takeaway 10

No one was safe in Russia except for the people in charge.

Analysis

Browder thought that as a citizen of the United States and as a lawyer, he was untouchable. He was wrong. Three of his lawyers also thought they were safe, that their positions and doing their legal duty for their clients would make them sacrosanct and safe from official abuse. They were wrong, but they realized in time and were able to get out of Russia. Magnitsky made the same mistake of believing that Russia had changed, that this was not like Stalinist times, that the Russian people would not stand for it, and that he could fight the system. He was wrong, and he paid with his life.

Key Takeaway 11

A measure of justice was possible, but not without great effort, difficulty, and risk.

Analysis

After years of lobbying the media and government officials, after years of fearing for his life and seeing people who tried to help him ending up dead under mysterious circumstances, and after being relentless, Browder was able to convince US Congressmen and Senators to consider a bill that was going to be called the Magnitsky Act that would punish the officials responsible by seizing their assets and depriving them of visas for travel. All kinds of domestic political issues got in the way, from ambitious would-be-secretaries of states to cattle rancher interests in Montana, but eventually the bill was passed resoundingly. The book ends with Browder and Magnitsky's widow and son in the audience at the European Parliament as an act similar to the Magnitsky act passed, showing the fruit of the labor of Browder's long struggle for Magnitsky.

Author's Style

Browder writes his story as a very fast paced, exciting tale, one that basically reads as a thriller. It is easy to imagine this being made into a film. He starts his story at the turning point, when he was held by Russian authorities in an airport before he was deported, then he takes the reader back to his childhood and all the way to how he ended up in this difficult situation. The second half of the book focuses on what he did after his airport incident, going to war with Putin's regime. The tone is very conversational, and Browder is not afraid to liven the book up with curse words. He is very effective at putting the reader inside his head, so that they feel they are experiencing things and his thoughts in the way he reacted to events as they unfolded.

Perspective

It is hard to claim that Browder is objective because he is a principal protagonist in the fight this book describes. He has a serious issue with the Putin regime, which almost ruined his life and business, then killed one of his friends. That being said, much of his story is verifiable by many credible newspapers and famous individuals. However, this book is a major salvo in a war between Browder and Putin's Russian government.

~~~~ END OF INSTAREAD ~~~~

Thank you for purchasing this Instaread book

Download the Instaread mobile app to get unlimited text & audio summaries of bestselling books.

Visit Instaread.co to learn more.